IMAGES
of England

AROUND
CALSTOCK PARISH

Cherry pickers, Harrowbarrow, 1920s. Market gardening brought properity to growers in Calstock parish during its peak from 1860 to 1970. The area became famous in the eighteenth century for its sweet black mazzard cherries, later early strawberries and spring flowers were successful market garden crops. On the left of this picture is Anna Langsford, behind her is Sidney Trewartha. On the right is Stanley Isobell, with Ida Hunt on his right. The man at the back is Mr Squance, and another member of the Langsford family is second from the left.

IMAGES
of England

AROUND
CALSTOCK PARISH

Calstock Archive Trust

TEMPUS

The River Tamar with its mines, 1932. The Tamar valley is famed for its beauty, but at the same time it has a strong industrial heritage. Mines like these at Gawton (left) and Okeltor (right) filled the river valley with smoke which brought thick fogs that endangered shipping. But they also brought tremendous prosperity and, ironically, new railways and roads that finally brought about the end of the river trade. The chimneys of Rumleigh Brickworks are beyond Gawton mine. Beside Okeltor are steep market gardens, and the track of the arsenic flue to the chimney up the hill can be made out. The walled garden at Harewood House is just visible. This picture also shows the flat marshy 'ham' fields bordering the river that were used by medieval farmers.

First published 2003

Tempus Publishing Limited
The Mill, Brimscombe Port,
Stroud, Gloucestershire, GL5 2QG

British Library Cataloguing in Publication Data.
A catalogue record for this book is available from the British Library.

ISBN 0 7524 2681 8

Typesetting and origination by Tempus Publishing Limited
Printed in Great Britain by Midway Colour Print, Wiltshire

Contents

Thomas Martyn map, 1748. This is one of the earliest maps to show Calstock parish in any detail. It's noticeable that unlike areas further west into Cornwall, the majority of place names are Early English rather than Celtic, showing that the area was one of the first parts of the county to be settled by the westward moving kingdom of Wessex from the seventh century onwards. The dotted lines across Hingston Down show the routes of old drovers' tracks, some of which are now roads. The turnpike road (now the A390) to the south of the Down had not been built when this map was surveyed. Symbols indicating tin and copper can be seen indicating mining areas of the time.

Introduction

Calstock parish nestles against the River Tamar as it curves and meanders from its source to the wider and straighter stretches of estuary close to Plymouth. The parish covers the same area as the ancient manor of Calstock – in medieval times the Duchy of Cornwall owned the manor, but it was already an ancient area. In 1086, the Domesday Book records that Calestoch or Kalestoc was held by William the Conqueror's brother – Robert, Count of Mortain – who had taken over from one Asgar. Like other parts of south-east Cornwall, place names in Calstock are largely early English rather than Celtic, indicating that it was settled by the Saxon/early Englishmen of Wessex, probably in the late seventh century after victories against the Celts in northern Cornwall. Stone, Bronze and Iron Age barrows on Hingston Down, a Stone Age beaker found at Harrowbarrow, and flint tools found at Gunnislake and Latchley show that people lived in or visited the area from the earliest times, and one theory is that the modern parish boundaries are identical to the boundaries of an ancient Celtic tref, which has merely changed hands as different administrative leaders took charge.

The modern parish includes the ancient villages of Albaston, Metherell and Harrowbarrow; Latchley with its early English strip fields; Chilsworthy; Gunnislake and St Ann's Chapel which developed alongside the Victorian mining boom; and Calstock Town itself. The story of the parish is inextricably linked with the River Tamar, which as well as providing food, gave the parish its main thoroughfare throughout its entire history until the twentieth century. Early settlers followed the river upstream, using the thickly wooded valley slopes for food and fuel, and lived on the edge of the higher land on Hingston Down, probably carrying out early farming on the south-facing slopes at Albaston, Metherell and Harrowbarrow, although traces of any old fields have been lost through later farming practices. There is map and field evidence of strip field patterns around Metherell, Harrowbarrow and Latchley, dating from around the seventh century and the arrival of the Saxon/early English people of Wessex.

The river is tidal as far as Weir Head at Gunnislake, and it was in this area that a medieval fish weir was built, at Hatches, which was also the site for a ferry crossing. West of Latchley was one of the oldest crossing points of the Tamar, a ford which was for centuries the lowest fordable point of the river, and an Iron Age fort in the woods above the crossing underlines its importance. It became less significant with the building of bridges at Horsebridge (in the neighbouring parish of Stoke Climsland) and New Bridge at Gunnislake in the fourteenth and fifteenth centuries. The river was used for taking produce to market and meant Calstock farmers could access a wider market for their produce – significantly the growing urban area of Plymouth, which was developing as a naval port from the fifteenth century onwards.

Calstock manor, sold by the Valletort family to Richard, Earl of Cornwall (brother of Henry III) in 1269, never had a manor house of its own. However, an unusually large and important estate developed at Cotehele, (from the Celtic *cuit* meaning wood and *hail* meaning estuary) – a ninety-acre freeholding at a time when most holdings were thirty acres or less, and held under conventional tenure. In 1337 Cotehele was held by Ralph, son of Ralph of Cotehele, passing to his sister Hilaria who married into the Edgcumbe family in 1353, a significant family in south-east Cornwall. Cotehele House was rebuilt between 1490 and 1520, and remained in the Edgcumbe family until it was given to the National Trust in 1947.

Calstock has been associated with mining throughout its history and was probably known for its minerals from the Iron Age. Early streaming methods were used to extract silver from Silver Valley above Harrowbarrow, and may have been used north of Hingston Down as well to extract tin and copper. During medieval times, lead and silver were carried across the river from mines at Bere Alston to be smelted at Calstock. A number of tin bounds were recorded from medieval times onwards in different parts of the parish. It wasn't until the development of steam pumping engines at the start of the nineteenth century that the area's mineral resources were exploited to a significant extent now that mining could be carried out at greater depths. The extensive copper mines that developed on the Devon bank of the Tamar at Devon Great Consols mine during the 1840s brought miners from West Cornwall in vast numbers. Exploratory mining took place all around the parish and villages expanded to deal with the growing population. The village of Gunnislake developed as a direct result of the mining boom. When Turner portrayed New Bridge at Gunnislake in his painting 'Crossing the Brook' of 1815, the village did not exist. Extensive building of typically terraced rows of miner's cottages took place through the middle years of the nineteenth century, to culminate in what is now the largest village in the parish. The mines of Calstock parish had mixed fortunes. Mines around Latchley, where it was hoped to find the copper and tin lodes from Devon Great Consols, had only limited success, but many other mines thrived, bringing prosperity to the valley until the price of copper fell at the end of the century. Among the most successful were Drakewalls, Okeltor, Prince of Wales mine at Harrowbarrow, Danescombe, and Clitters mine at Dimson.

Alongside the mines, the infrastructure of the area improved. Roads, many of which were steep, rutted mud tracks impassable in winter, were looked after and metalled. The East Cornwall Mineral Railway, and eventually the line between Calstock and Plymouth, improved communications. A local farmer, James Walter Lawry, found that he could use the new railway to send strawberries to Covent Garden market, and the market gardening industry of the Tamar Valley took off. The valley had long been famous for its black cherries, or mazzards, and soft fruit from south-facing fruit gardens in Calstock parish was taken to Plymouth and Devonport markets by river. But the early ripening fruit from Calstock and the rest of the valley could be sold at Covent Garden at a premium price before fruit from other parts of the country was available, and, as the fortunes of the mines waned, many people turned to market gardening. Early strawberries, other soft fruit, and, later, spring bulbs (mainly daffodils) and anemones were the main crops grown. The first greenhouses in the area were put up at market gardens around Calstock Town, which became well known for their very sweet flavoured tomatoes. The Tamar again was a vital element of the industry, with people taking produce to Plymouth and Devonport markets by river until the railway viaduct was completed in 1907.

The market gardening industry thrived until competition from foreign markets made it unprofitable in the 1960s and 1970s. Some of Calstock's mines were re-worked during the First and Second World Wars, for wolfram and manganese to help with weapons production. During the Second World War, many people from Plymouth stayed in various places around the parish to escape the blitz on the Dockyard. Nowadays, a majority of the working population of the parish travel into Plymouth each day to work.

The villages of Calstock parish retain some of the community spirit that has been with them throughout their history. Music and sporting activities have always played their part, and even though many older people feel the heart of the community has been lost, some community events hold echoes of the rich heritage of the area's history.

This book was compiled by members of Calstock Archive Trust

One
The River Tamar

Windings of the River Tamar. The River Tamar meanders and winds its way towards Plymouth. This postcard was sent to Arthur Down of Exeter from someone called Bert. It shows one of the paddle steamers which were used by Calstock people to get to market, and by city dwellers from Plymouth for outings up the river. Cotehele Woods are on the right hand side, and the roof of the Ashburton (now Danescombe) Hotel can be seen.

Weir Head, 1880. This was the highest navigable point of the Tamar and the only place in the immediate vicinity where paddle steamers, like the SS *Alexandra* in this picture, could turn. The chimneys of Bealeswood Brickworks are visible in the background. The lock for the 'Tamar Manure Navigation Canal', completed in 1808, is just behind the steamer. It enabled barges to access the quay at Newbridge, the brickworks and to take coal to Gunnislake gasworks.

The Weir near Calstock

The Ferry, Gunnislake.

Gunnislake Ferry, 1920s. The lock-keeper of the Manure Navigation Canal provided a ferry service between Gunnislake and the Devon bank, for access to the thriving copper and tin port of Morwellham. Nearby was an old quay called Netstakes, so called because salmon fishermen hung their nets on poles to dry, as can be seen in the photograph. The original and ancient ferry service ran from here to the Devon bank, although it became less important after Newbridge was built in about 1520.

Opposite below: The weir and fish trap, near Calstock. Old maps of Calstock show a number of weirs, spelt 'ware', which were probably the sites of fish weirs. The history of this fish weir is well documented from medieval times onwards, and the area is also known as Hatches, from the salmon trap or hatch on the left. For hundreds of years Tavistock Abbey owned the fish weir, and the Abbot exerted a strict control over salmon fishing in the Tamar, and there were frequent disputes. One Calstock man was charged with allowing the logs he was floating downstream to smash through the weir.

Children at Ferry Cottage, Gunnislake, early 1900s. Albert and Emily Teague, Harwood's children, are pictured outside their home on the Island at Gunnislake. The wheelbarrow was probably a home-made toy.

Calstock Ferry, early twentieth century. Calstock Town was also the site of a very old ferry, operated until 1935 by the tenant of Ferry Farm opposite Calstock, then by the Goss family whose shipyard was next to the farm. Before the railway viaduct was built, people used the ferry to get to Bere Alston on the Devon side of the river, to work in the mines and market gardening fields.

39089

The Ferry and Goss Shipyard, 1904. Ferry Farm was run as an inn for the latter half of the nineteenth century and early twentieth century, claiming to be the oldest licensed 'house' in Devon. It catered for up to 200 visitors a time off the paddle-steamer pleasure trips, and served a celebrated strawberry and cream tea. From the early 1900s until 1935 the farm developed its dairy herd, selling prize-winning bottled milk. To the right of the picture is the Goss Shipyard.

Doug Langsford, Calstock ferryman, 1968. Maude Frampton was the last person to use the Calstock Ferry crossing to Ferry Farm. At that time Doug Langsford, the ferryman, operated an hourly service, combining this with cleaning the streets and toilets, at a weekly wage of £5. In recent years a new ferry service has been set up between Calstock and Cotehele House, lower down the Cornish bank, and to Morwellham Quay.

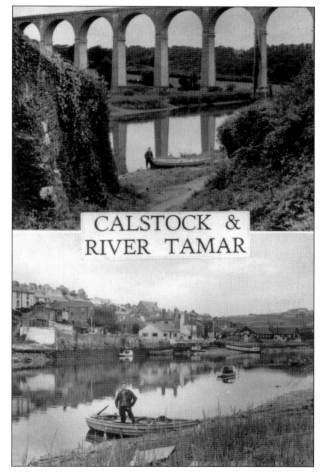

CALSTOCK &
RIVER TAMAR

Sailing barge, Sirdar, at Morwell Rocks, *c.* 1900. Sailing barges were the main form of transport for people in Calstock parish for hundreds of years. Although this one is in full sail, it was common for the crew to pole the boat along the bank, making use of the changing tides to help take the vessel up or down stream. Most barges until the mid-nineteenth century were open decked, and were unwieldy. But they were extremely valuable – in the 1675 will of Andrew Summers, a Calstock bargeman, his boat and equipment was valued at £30 – a considerable amount at the time.

Tom Old Snr, *c.* 1880. Tom Old, who was born in 1858, was a Calstock bargeman. He started his working life on the *Thomasine*, before becoming mate of the *Edith* for twenty-two years, and then Master of the *Shamrock* for fourteen years. He was also Master on the *Sirdar*. The bargemen often spent all week away from home, plying their trade in the Tamar, Plymouth and neighbouring coastal ports. His son, Tom Old Jnr, wrote, 'I think of my father as a typical bargeman, as Shakespeare's Old Gobbo would say "an honest exceeding poor man."'

Tug at Calstock. Steam power and later diesel engines were a great boon for the Tamar sailing barges. The boats would sometimes have to be poled around the sharp bends below Calstock, but once powered tugs arrived, the sailing barges would hitch a tow upstream – sometimes as many as three or four being pulled behind a tug.

Tom Old Jnr, *c.* 1900. Tom Old Jnr became a well-known Methodist minister, training in America and graduating in North Dakota in 1921. He returned to Cornwall and joined the Methodist circuit in Liskeard and Helston.

The viaduct nears completion, 1906. Children in their Sunday best may be waiting at Calstock Quay for a trip on the steamer. The outside ship is thought to be the Eleanor. The viaduct was completed in 1907, linking the railway from Gunnislake and Calstock with Bere Alston and Bere Ferrers and giving access to the main line to London. This gradually brought about the demise of the river trade.

Kelly Quay and the incline. The incline railway, which carried ore from the East Cornwall Mineral Railway down to the quay, can be seen to the left of the picture; at its foot is a lime kiln. In the foreground the barges are moored alongside Perry & Spear's yard – a firm of agricultural and coal merchants that also operated from Kelly Bray, Gunnislake and Tavistock stations and from Halton Quay. Calstock was a busy port; on census day in 1881 six schooners and two barges were listed – a typical day. On the far left is the Ashburton (now Danescombe Valley) Hotel, built in 1859.

Gurt 'oss, early 1900s. The quays of Calstock were never graced by a steam engine to move trucks from the incline, or the viaduct hoist, to the quays. They were always moved by a succession of large horses – each known locally as the 'gurt 'oss'.

A day out on the river. From the 1840s a fleet of paddle steamers, the *Alert*, *Pheonix*, *Queen* and *Empress*, offered passenger and excursion services on the Tamar, and when the tides were right, up to a thousand sightseers would enjoy the trip up to Calstock. In 1856 Queen Victoria and her family travelled by steamer to Morwellham and onwards to visit Endsleigh House, country home of the Duke of Bedford. In Calstock there was much dismay at the 'habitual practice of drunkenness' often associated with the pleasure trips.

Western Belle at Calstock, 1960s. The *Western Belle* was used by the Millbrook Steamboat Company for river trips from Plymouth to Calstock in the period after the Second World War. The journey took four hours, and people would either stay on board for the return journey, or go back to Plymouth on the train. The *Western Belle* originally had small round portholes, which had to be replaced under safety regulations with large rectangular windows that could be used for escape if necessary.

Latchley Weir. This weir was built to supply the Great Leat at Devon Great Consols mine, completed in 1849. Water held back by the weir was fed into the two miles of leat which then supplied a pair of 40ft water wheels that pumped water from three shafts of the mine. The weir was blown up in 1925 to improve salmon fishing.

Salmon fishing, Cotehele. Fishing in the River Tamar was for centuries a vital source of food, and in Victorian times provided wealthy landowners with a country sport. In a court case of 1612 a local farmer, Walter Adam, confirmed he had caught 200 salmon and many other fish in the Tamar, the value of each salmon being 18d. Although a few fishermen are still licensed to catch salmon, and anglers still frequent the river's banks, only a handful of fish have been caught in recent years.

The *Charlotte Rose* at Cotehele, 1972. The quay at Cotehele was used in the filming of the television programme *The Onedin Line*, bringing a number of ships including the *Charlotte Rose* up the Tamar for the event.

Two
Calstock Mines

Okeltor Mine in operation, 1880s. This, and the following rare mining photographs which are around 100 years old, are some of the very few to show the East Cornwall mines with mining equipment in situ. In its heyday, Okeltor was one of the most important mines on the edge of Calstock village. Passengers on paddle-steamer outings were fascinated to watch the busy workings during trips up the river.

Okeltor Mine, c. 1890. This photograph was taken shortly after Okeltor closed in 1887. The mine produced 213 tons of black tin and 13,215 tons of copper. Arsenic was produced in later years and a small amount of lead also came from the mine. In its final year sixty-two men were employed underground, with eighty working at the surface. A special quay was built below its slopes, capable of taking vessels of up to 200 tons, to save the cost of hauling ore by horse to Calstock.

Miners at Danescombe Mine, late 1890s. The miners appear to be dressed in their best clothes for the occasion, but unfortunately the bal maidens, on the left, cannot be clearly seen. Several members of the Wilton and Philp families have been identified, and somewhere on the right is William Bant, famous for his entombment in Drakewalls Mine in 1889. Danescombe Valley Mine was worked as part of Calstock Consols for copper and silver lead. At its height, between 1847 and 1858, more than 3,000 tons of copper ore was raised.

Stamps at the Prince of Wales Mine, Harrowbarrow, c. 1910. Thirty-six heads of stamps were used to crush the ore at the Prince of Wales Mine. It was originally worked for copper, but became an important tin mine, working together with others in the area to produce arsenic, lead and silver from the complex lodes.

Pumping engine at Watson's Shaft, Prince of Wales Mine, c. 1910. A fifty-inch cylinder engine was installed in 1879 to keep the mine pumped dry. At its height 200 people were employed. It closed in 1914, although the mine waste and adits were worked during the Second World War to extract minerals, to help produce munitions.

Captain Murton at Hingston Down Mine. William Murton, a mine captain, lived at Clitters Mine below Chilsworthy from around 1901 to 1923. He visited other mines in the area, as far as Kit Hill, in his pony and trap. This photograph shows Bailey's Shaft, the engine house of which still stands today. The overhead pipe is probably taking away the water that has been pumped from the shaft.

Wheal Arthur Headgear, 1940s. Wheal Arthur, to the north of Calstock at Slimeford, and close to the Tamar, began working in 1850 on lodes producing arsenic, copper, pitchblende, iron, lead, tin and wolfram. For part of its history it was worked together with the neighbouring Wheal Edward. Operations continued sporadically until 1926, and the waste was worked for wolfram during the Second World War.

Michael's Shaft, Old Gunnislake Mine, early twentieth century. Started in the 1770s, Old Gunnislake was developed by John Williams of Scorrier near Redruth. He built cottages for the miners below Dimson, which was known as Williams' Town, and later grew into Gunnislake.

Water wheel at Wheal Benny Mine, early 1900s. Wheal Benny was one of the few mines to rely entirely on water power to pump water out of its lower levels. The wheel pit for the 36ft wheel is still visible in Greenscombe Woods to the west of Latchley, together with the arsenic calciner (processor) and buddles used to help separate metals from the ore. The mine produced tin, arsenic, and, during the First World War, a certain amount of wolfram, before finally closing in 1928.

Miners at Bedford United, *c.* 1923. Most of the men employed by this mine on the Devon side of the Tamar came from Gunnislake. From left to right, back row: Sid Hitchins, Alf Wilcocks, Stan Isobel, George Perkins, Albert Davy, Mr Allen. Front row: -?-, Charlie Allen, -?-, Stan Cory, Mr Allen, Sam Marshall, Lou Allen. The mine opened in 1840 on the Marquis lode, and between 1844 and 1856 more than 21,000 tons of copper were raised, paying dividends of £36,000, making the mine the third largest copper producer in Devon. It closed in 1925, and in its latter years arsenic, wolfram, tin and iron ore were produced.

Opposite below: Boys from Gunnislake in Montana. This is one of many groups of miners who sent back pictures of themselves to their families. Some succeeded in making money at the New World mines, and there are houses with names like Klondike around the parish. For others the hard work thousands of miles from home brought only limited success, and some miners were killed in mine accidents. Sometimes the family would travel out to join their husbands and fathers, but quite often men would stay abroad for only a few years before returning.

Emigration office, Gunnislake, 1912. By the end of the nineteenth century virtually all mining in Calstock parish had come to an end. Copper prices had plummeted and even the arsenic trade, which had kept many mines in business, was tailing off. Unemployment brought poverty, and news of profitable mines in America, Canada, Australia, South Africa, as well as Spain and Norway attracted the out-of-work miners. Mr Bowhay, of the wealthy Albaston family, often loaned the fares for the journey, which were purchased from Jeremiah Youlton's shipping office. This photograph, dated March 1912, shows, from the left: J. Youlton, Mr Darcy, William Wake, Mr Youlton, J. Saunders, C. Eva. William Wake was one of several local men who paid £10 10s for passage on the ill-fated *Titanic*, others were Frederick Pengelly, William Wake, Harry and Shadrach Gale, and George Green.

Three
Railway

East Cornwall Mineral Railway, *c*. 1903. With the growth of mining in the Calstock area there was a need to improve transportation between the mines and the quays on the Tamar. The 3ft 6ins gauge East Cornwall Mineral Railway was opened to goods traffic only on 7 May 1872. At Butts, above Calstock, ore was taken down an incline tramroad to the quays, and coal was hauled up for transportation back to the mines and brickworks that lined the route. This is an early engine of the Mineral Railway, with the open carriages that were typical of the time. In 1908 the narrow gauge was converted to standard gauge to link with the newly-built Calstock viaduct line.

Engine at junction to Hingston Quarry, mid-1950s. This Ivatt LMS262 engine is passing the siding for Hingston Down Quarry.

Sarah Jenkyn, railway mistress at Latchley Halt, around 1910. Sarah Jenkyn moved to the station at the age of six months, and lived there until 1979, when she was eighty-seven. She was one of the few female station mistresses in the country. The children are Dorothy and Lesley Woolcock, with their father Frank behind. The advertisements on the wall promote the delights of Southampton, London and Paris, although Paris must have been an unlikely destination for the miners, farmers and market gardeners of Calstock in the early twentieth century.

Wire pulleys, known as Blondins, at work on the construction of Calstock Viaduct, c. 1905. Joining the railway from Calstock to Bere Alston required a major engineering project – the building of Calstock Viaduct. The two wires strung across the river were nicknamed 'Blondins' after the French tightrope walker, Jean Francois Gravelet. They were used to move pre-shaped concrete blocks into place as the viaduct pillars were built up.

Derailed engine, *Blanche*, 1907. When work started on Calstock Viaduct, rails and stones were brought to the site by horse and cart. Later the engine *Blanche* was hired to haul heavy loads, enabling the new railway to progress more quickly. She was derailed near the Harewood crossing during the work shortly before the viaduct opened.

View along Calstock Viaduct, 1907. The ambitious engineering project is nearly at an end, and this view shows why such a high structure was needed to join the railway line from Calstock to Bere Alston. The pile of soil and small stones in the foreground formed a buttress to help support the start of the viaduct on the Devon side.

The opening of Calstock Station, 2 March 1908. A crowd has gathered at Calstock Station for the opening of the long-awaited line. It was particularly advantageous to Calstock market gardeners who were able to send their produce directly by railway from stations in Calstock parish to London and the Midlands. Previously, produce had to be taken by road or river to Saltash or Bere Alston to be transferred to rail wagons.

Engine *Lord St Levan* at Chilsworthy station, 1908. The weekly trip to market from stations like Chilsworthy, Latchley and Gunnislake gave many of the women in the villages a much-appreciated day out. In 1908 special market day fares were advertised for Thursdays and Saturdays. A third-class return to Devonport cost 1s 8d, and passengers were allowed to carry up to 60lbs of marketing goods free of charge. They must have had strong arms!

Great Western Bus, St Ann's Chapel, 1905. The Great Western Railway operated a motor bus between the Calstock area and Saltash before the viaduct was built. It enabled passengers to join GWR trains, which reached Saltash over the Royal Albert Bridge built by Brunel in 1859. This postcard was sent by Dr Tom Bowhay, the local GP, to his sister Florence who was in Portugal at the time.

Bernard Muggeridge taking croust in the 1950s. Bernard Muggeridge was a driver for the Southern Railway and a well-known figure at the stations in the parish. Here he is enjoying his lunch or 'croust' – a pasty.

Gunnislake station staff, June 1950. From left to right, back row: John Snell, clerk; Rex Phillips, signalman; Jock Thompson, porter. Front row: George Symes, porter/signalman, Ron Pote, porter/signalman, George Jury, signalman.

Four
Market Gardening

Enjoying the mazzards, 1920s. The Tamar Valley was famous from the eighteenth century for its sweet black cherries, known as mazzards. Here, a very young Laureen Reynolds is enjoying the fruit with her aunt, Joyce Cundy, on the right. Carriers from all over Devon and Cornwall would travel by cart to collect the cherries and take them to market. One of them, Grace Hitchens, died in 1869 at the age of ninety-one after her fifty-mile journey from St Dominick to collect cherries to take to Redruth market.

Steep market garden land bordering the Tamar. Market gardening gave Calstock growers a good income, particularly in the early days, from 1860 onwards, when they were able to get premium prices for their early fruiting strawberries, but it was hard work. The fields had to be worked by hand, and many were extremely steep, with gradients of up to 1 in 1.5. However, with the river water keeping temperatures warm, southern slopes benefiting from plenty of sunlight, and eastern slopes enjoying shelter from the winds, soft fruit crops were good. These fields at Danescombe were valued south-east-facing land, and were close to the quays for sending the produce to market.

Cherry ladders at Harrowbarrow, 1950s. Cherry ladders could be as long as fifty feet to reach the tops of the tall cherry trees, which were grafted on to wild rootstock. Climbing them was a nerve-racking process; at this farm on one occasion a pig got stuck under the bottom rung of a ladder, to the consternation of the picker high above. Simply moving the ladder from one branch to another required a certain amount of skill – and strength. Picking cherries was another skill, because careless picking could damage the bud for the following year's crop. In the fruit shed, the cherries would be checked, twigs removed and the fruit packed into large chip baskets to take to market.

Market garden workers, Harrowbarrow, 1914/15. These workers were employed on Arnold Jope's market garden, rented from the Edgcumbe estate near Cotehele. From left to right: Bessie Damerel, ? Medland, Olive Fletcher, Susan Damerel, Sam Hunn, Arnold Jope, ? Gale. The women are using bowhoes, used for weeding between strawberry plants, and the men are wielding 'viskeys' – the local name for a mattock used for breaking up the ground.

Strawberry pickers, early 1900s. Picking the fruit for market was a job that involved the whole family. It often meant a very early start in the morning to gather fresh fruit for the 6.00 a.m. train. Polly Beer, in the centre of this photograph, seems to be carrying a dish, perhaps of lunch. She is pictured with her second husband, Mr Causeway, and his three daughters from his first marriage, one of whom was named Cora.

Strawberry pickers at Paul's fruit gardens, Danescombe, early 1900s. Casual labour, as well as the extended family, would be called upon to help out at picking time. One local woman remembers earning 3d for an evening's picking work – money that helped to pay for 'anniversary' clothes. The punnets shown in the boxes in the front of this picture are round – early punnets were circular, but later were made rectangular to ease packing in the crates.

Strawberry pickers at Whimple Farm, Gunnislake, 1910. Mr Harris, owner of Whimple Farm, with his workers and a crop of strawberries. The fruit is packed in 2lb large 'chip' baskets, of the later rectangular design. Making the punnets during the winter provided many families with a welcome income when market gardening work was unavailable.

Strawberry boxes, Harrowbarrow, early twentieth century. Boxes of punnets could be sent by train, and picking was often done early in the morning to be sold in London the same day. The early Tamar Valley strawberries got good prices in London, Birmingham, Manchester and Scotland. Bracken was packed around the punnets to keep them steady and to stop the fruit from being bruised.

Lizzie Walters selling strawberries, c. 1950. Lizzie Walters used to sit at the corner of the street in Calstock selling fruit and other produce. Behind her is a blackboard advertising river trips on board the *Tamar Belle*.

Market garden workers with rejected flowers. Daffodils became a major source of income for the Calstock and Tamar Valley market gardeners. These men, working for George Craddick, are gathering up a load of flowers that have been discarded. It could be that the price at market was low, making it uneconomical to send them. Growers would receive telegrams from wholesalers at markets in London, Birmingham, Manchester, Edinburgh and Glasgow informing them of prices and urging them to send produce by train.

Flower boxes at Calstock station, April 1955. The railway was vital to the market gardening industry, enabling growers to get their produce quickly to market, and the market gardeners were vital to the Calstock, Gunnislake, Chilsworthy and Latchley stations, keeping the platforms full of produce, particularly in the spring and summer. These flower boxes will be loaded on the next train by Albert Harris and Frank Chard. The railway and the market gardening industry died together, with Latchley and Chilsworthy stations closing in the 1960s.

Kimberley Jam Factory, early 1900s. Tamar Valley growers depended on the premium prices they could get for their fruit which ripened two weeks earlier than elsewhere in the country. As soon as crops elsewhere were available they would tell their workers to 'pick for jam'. The Kimberley jam factory at St Ann's Chapel on the left-hand side was one of several small jam producers in the valley, although most was packed in barrels and sent to Plymouth or further afield. The van in front is from Skinnards Bakery, Albaston.

Transporting apples to market, 1920s. This van is loaded with sacks full of cider apples. Most farms in Calstock parish had at least two acres of orchard. Many also had cider pounds, or a share in a pound in the village. During the eighteenth century, cider was part of the wage for a farm labourer. Some local cider apple varieties, such as Pig's Snout, are being grafted and preserved. Bob Watson is leaning against the cab.

Orchards at Bitthams, Chilsworthy, 1920s. Pictured are Morley Rogers, Herbert Stenlake and Alfred Stenlake preparing to climb a ladder and pick at orchards at Bitthams. Even the north-facing slopes in Latchley and Chilsworthy were planted with every kind of soft fruit bush and tree to take advantage of the thriving market gardening industry. Farmers ran 'mixed' farms, combining market gardening with a little bit of dairy, poultry and pigs.

Girls at Calstock Chip Basket Factory, 1954. Making the 'chips' or punnets for the soft fruit grown by Calstock market gardeners was originally done during the winter by local women in their cottages. Calstock Chip Basket Factory was set up in the 1920s and traded as Tamar Valley & District Chip Basket and Box Making Factory. Initially, thirty women and twelve men were employed under the manager, Mr Billings, with the women earning 10s a week for making 10 gross of baskets a day. Standing in front of large 'chips' are, left to right, back row: Julie Start, Rhona Dodderidge, Pam Bampton, Pam Holman, Ariel Doidge. Kath Deanand and Rose westlake are in the front row.

Chip factory lumberman, 1925. Timber came from the woodlands at Gulworthy and also from the New Forest, from Worcester and from Canada. Tom Walters was one of the lumbermen, who would cut the wood into different lengths; then the bark was removed and the logs were passed through a peeling machine.

Paul Walters, Alf Howe and Tony Royston inside Calstock Chip Factory, 1950. The strips of peeled wood were plaited into baskets. The baskets were then dried in the sunshine or in a heated room. The handles were then put on and the completed baskets tied into bundles ready for despatch by rail or lorry.

Calstock Chip Factory, 1980s. This building, originally a brickworks, offered sterilising facilities for bulb growers as well as housing the chip basket-making factory. Daffodils were widely grown by the parish's market gardeners, but were vulnerable to infestations of eelworms. To counter this, bulbs were lifted each summer, and sterilised in hot water, before being replanted for the next year's crop. The girl in this photograph is Catherine Goss, and it was taken shortly before the chip factory was demolished in 1985.

Five
Agriculture

Hearn's Dairy, 1908. Farmers had to find their own markets for their produce and, although many took their milk, butter and cream to Devonport and Plymouth markets using the market boat from one of the many quays on the Tamar, it was better to set up a delivery round. Alfred Owen Hearn farmed at Cox Park, but had a delivery round in Gunnislake.

Haymaking. Bill May, Jack Langsford, Bill Rich and Aydon Langsford are taking a rest during haymaking at Harrowbarrow.

Making a hayrick at Latchley Plain, 1920s. Tom Sobey, a farmer at Latchley Plain, stands on top of his hayrick, helped by Morley 'Star' Rogers, on the right. It was common for farmers within an area to help each other out at busy times of the year.

Roger Croad shows off his tractor, 1960s. Mechanisation was slow to come to Calstock parish, and before the Second World War there were very few motor vehicles, let alone tractors. In the 1950s farmers were encouraged to buy tractors. Mechanisation brought huge changes; not least, it showed up the difficulties of tractors working the steep market gardens bordering the Tamar, which traditionally had been dug, hoed and planted by hand.

Thresher on the move, 1960s. Roger Croad is towing Tom Sobey's thresher towards Latchley village. These machines, originally steam-driven, travelled from farm to farm during the season. In Latchley it was set up behind a large barn in the village centre to thresh corn for all the farmers in the village. By the 1960s steam was no longer used, and the thresher ran from the power-take-off from the tractor.

Early combine, 1950s. This early combine harvester is being used in fields at Harrowbarrow.

Six

Quarrying and
Other Industry

Cutting granite at Kit Hill Quarry, early 1900s. Granite workers from Calstock parish used skills learnt at quarries at Gunnislake and on Hingston Down in their work at Kit Hill Quarry, where the quarrymen were thought of as kings of their trade. Granite from Gunnislake and Kit Hill was used for buildings and as ornamental stone throughout the south of England, and the elvan stone from Hingston Down was used for road making.

Pearsons Quarry at Gunnislake, *c.* 1880. Now completely overgrown, Pearson's Quarry employed 700 men by the end of the nineteenth century, its granite used at Devonport Dockyard for fortifications around Plymouth, and in London at Blackfriar's Bridge, in Hammersmith, Kensington and Chelsea. A railway track was built to take the granite to Gunnislake station. The quarry closed in 1914.

Snowden's Quarry at Gunnislake, *c.* 1880. With its location beside the Tamar, Snowden's Quarry had easy access to river barges. Its stone was mostly used for road building. Plymouth Brickworks can be seen at the top of the picture, and the chimneys of Greenhill Arsenic Works are to the left.

Granite setts ready to load at Kelly Quay, 1904. The granite setts on the quayside are ready for loading and transporting to Dover, on the steam ship *Albion*. One of the largest contracts awarded to Pearson's Quarry was the job of supplying stone for the breakwater at Dover. This picture shows the view from Kelly Quay towards Calstock before the viaduct was built.

Gunnislake Bone Mill at Weir Head, 1890. This unnamed Edwardian family may have had something to do with the bone mill in the background. The mill was advertised for sale in 1811 as 'well adapted for corn, iron, hammer, or rolling copper'. It became the Tamar Paper Mill from about 1851-1876. It reopened in 1879 as the Tamar Bone Mills and General Stores, grinding bone, barley and maize and selling fertilisers and animal feed until 1905. It finally closed in 1927.

Gunnislake Gas Works, 1880. The *Daily Western Mercury* of Saturday 2 March 1872 reported the festivities on the previous Wednesday evening when the gas works started to produce gas. They had hoped to light up the village by six, but it was nearly seven before the lights 'assumed brilliancy'. The new Gas Works, built by Hawke & Venning Ltd, provided street lighting, but by December 1874 the village could not pay for the service. £20 had been collected for the lights, with £10 spent on gas, but the village stayed in darkness for two years, until it was agreed to spend up to £42 a year to provide the lights.

Carpentry apprentices working at Metherell, *c.* 1910. Richard Matthews, on the left, and Sidney Trewartha, were apprenticed to Risdens at Metherell, learning the skills of wheelwrights and undertakers.

Goss Yard workers, early 1900s. The Goss shipyard at Calstock was the best known of several small boatyards, producing many of the sailing barges that plied their trade up and down the Tamar. The Garlandstone, a Goss-built barge, is now at Morwellham Quay, but no longer sails. This took several years to complete, as work was only done when repair work was slow. James Goss is in the centre of the picture with his sons Harry (right) and Louis (left). Tom Goss is on the right of the front row.

Knitting factory Harrowbarrow, 1920s. Roseberry Cottage in Harrowbarrow once housed a small knitting factory. Among other things, the workers knitted socks for soldiers during the First World War. These employees taking a break are, from left to right, back row: Olive Hamley (née Spear), Olive Hunn (née Lee), Gladys Trebilcock (née Brown), Meta Allen (née Clymo). Front row: Doris Santo (née Gale), Kathleeen Lampen (née Congdon), Carrie Matthews (née Rich), Flo Doney. Muriel Gale remembers as a small child being asked to take a message to her sister at the knitting factory, and she can remember rooms full of knitting machines, upstairs and downstairs, in the small cottage. Roseberry Cottage is now well-known in the area for the models of mine buildings and other village houses that has been set up in its garden.

Seven
Religion

Band of Hope, Latchley, 1905. Mining brought prosperity to the Calstock area, but it also brought problems. There was increasing concern in late Victorian times about drunkenness and the violence that often accompanied it. Most villages had their own 'Band of Hope' to encourage abstinence and warn of the dangers of alcohol. Latchley trebled in size with the influx of miners, and at one stage boasted three inns among its fifty or so houses. Its notoriety spread in 1860 when two miners fought for two hours following an argument at the Rising Sun Inn. John Bodiner died as a result of his injuries, and the subsequent newspaper article in the *Cornish Times* was unequivocal: 'Amongst a mining population outrages frequently occur, and unhappily of a diabolical character. Drunkenness and vice abound to a fearful extent, and a taste for the low and vulgar in every sense is to be witnessed at all times and at all seasons'. The chimney in the background belonging to Latchley Consols Mine no longer stands. Jack Truscott is leading this Band of Hope.

Band of Hope, Calstock, early 1900s. The Band of Hope movement grew concurrently with Methodist chapels. Members would meet regularly, usually at the chapel, and would often parade through the village, singing hymns. Calstock Band of Hope is marching down Fore Street, past the Boot Inn. Charles Williams is playing the drums, Hartley Morton the side drums, Charlie Trewin the cornet, Sam Preston the tenor horn, Alfred Preston the euphonium and Norman Cox is playing the tenor horn wearing a check cap.

Opposite below: New Bridge Chapel, Gunnislake, *c.* 1900. The mining industry had another effect on the area – in 1863 the original Bible Christian Chapel was deemed to be dangerous because of mining operations. A new one was built against the steep hillside above Newbridge, the builder was Mr Knight and the pastor at the time was Reverend Clarke. In more recent times, large holes that have opened in gardens in Gunnislake show the long-term effects of the mining industry. This picture, from an old directory, is the only close-up image of the chapel that remains.

Salvation Army concert, 1934-35. The Salvation Army was also popular in Calstock villages for its message of abstinence, and for its bands and singing. From left to right, seated in front are: K. Tippet, Una Southcott, Pam Southcott, -?-, Roy Tippett. Kneeling: Norman Strong, Rose Vinard, Joan Brailey, Dots Pote, Marjorie Williams, -?-, Pearl Higman, R. Ley. Adults seated: -?-, Fred Leseelleur, Winnie Leseelleur, -?-. First row: -?-, Mrs. Strong, -?-, Alice Hill (Brent), Agnes Haddy, Mrs Southcott, Mrs Geake, -?-, Annie Penny, Mrs Brailey, -?-, -?-. Back row: -?-, -?-, Mrs Haddy, -?-, -?-, -?-, Let Ferris, Ron Bratchley, -?-, Lewis Sanders.

Laying the Foundation Stone for Mount Zion Chapel, Calstock, 17 July 1909. Victorian Calstock was more 'chapel' than 'church' and at one stage had three non-conformist chapels, including the old Mount Zion Chapel, opened in 1856. When the village's Bible Christian Chapel closed in 1890, its members joined the congregation at Mount Zion, which became cramped, necessitating the construction of a new Mount Zion Chapel. Occasions such as this were an opportunity for people to appear in their best clothes, and these delightful, unposed photographs reveal them in all their finery. No doubt the tea that followed, held in the new schoolroom beneath the church was an added attraction.

Opening of Mount Zion Chapel, Calstock, 1910. The new Mount Zion Chapel was opened in 1910. People went to chapel in the morning and evening on Sunday, and children also went to Sunday school. The chapel building is now the home of a local organisation, the Peterloo Poets. The Reverend Tom Old, who treasured and kept these two old photographs, wrote of his memories of 'meetings of protest about Leopold's treatment of the people of the Congo' and 'other social and semi-political causes on which we were united'.

Harvest Festival at old Mount Zion Chapel, Calstock, early 1900s. Gas lamps help to light up the abundant harvest festival offerings at the old Mount Zion Chapel, which closed in 1910. The chapel became St Andrew's Hall and has now been converted into a house.

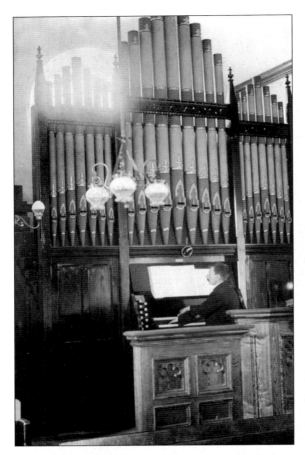

Mount Zion organ. The organist, Mr Bickle, shows off the organ at the new Mount Zion Chapel. Mr Bickle was choir leader and conductor, and also sold musical instruments at his tailor and draper's shop in Calstock.

Mount Zion choir. The choir is photographed at Harvest Festival at the new Mount Zion Chapel. Chapel was a place for a social get-together as well as for worship. Members of a Chapel would meet at neighbouring chapels for Harvest Festivals and concerts.

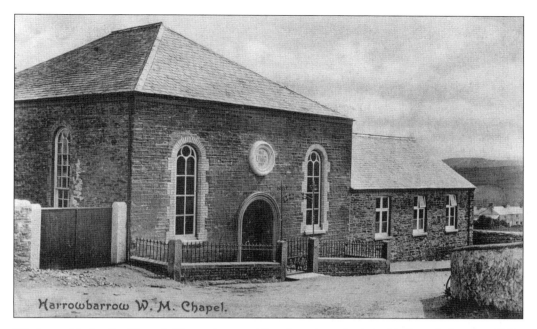

Wesleyan Methodist Chapel, Harrowbarrow. The chapel was built in 1842, and closed in 1991, and has now been converted into a private home.

Sisterhood, Methodist Chapel, *c.* 1990. Regular meetings of the Sisterhood were held at the Methodist Chapel for hymns and talks. From left to right, front row: Doris Watts, Bertha Pickersgill, Nancy Symons, Alice Williams. Second row: Florence Burgoyne, Audrey Collins, Charlie Pickersgill. Ida Duke is in the middle of the third row, and Mrs Holmes is on the right of the back row.

Harvest Festival, Metherell Baptist Church, pre-1939. Autumn celebrations gave neighbouring chapels another opportunity for a social event. Chapelgoers would go to Harvest Festival at 11 a.m., then visit neighbouring events later in the day.

Interior of Latchley Chapel. The miners in the village paid for the magnificent organ at Latchley Methodist Chapel. An earlier chapel became the Sunday school, when this chapel was built in 1866 to deal with the larger population. The chapel was a centre of community life, with villagers often attending chapel at Latchley in the morning and walking through the woods to Luckett Chapel for the evening service.

Latchley Church in the snow. Thomas Hullah, vicar at Calstock Church in the second half of the nineteenth century, set about trying to counter the influence of the Methodist Church in his parish. He wrote that Latchley was a 'distant region' in his parish, 'Hemmed in between the river and Hingston Down, which rises rapidly to 700 feet above it, it is only approachable by the steepest and worst of roads, and therefore very difficult of access'. He was approached by a villager who told him that Latchley villagers found it hard to walk the four miles to Calstock Church. For three years, Church of England services were held in a barn behind a farm until, in 1882, St Michael and All Angel's Chapel of Ease was completed at a cost of £1,147. Thomas Hullah also arranged for new Church of England places of worship to be built at Gunnislake, St Ann's Chapel and Harrowbarrow.

Chilsworthy choir outside the Methodist Chapel, 1920. Chapelgoers throughout the parish would travel between the chapels on Sundays for different services, and would join their colleagues for celebrations such as Anniversary Tea. From left to right, back row: A. Ridholls, C. Harding, W.H. Philip, M.J. Stenlake, R. Short, W.Haimes. Middle row: R. Woolcocks, B. Stenlake, J. Burley, L. Stenlake, M. Haimes, E. Penney, M. Harding, L. Ridholls, Alfred Hearn. Front row: B. Harding, K. Harris, R. Short, K. Rodda, L. Hearn, F.Toye, K. Reynolds.

Calstock Church, early 1900s. For centuries all Calstock parishioners were required to walk to Church at Calstock Churchtown every Sunday. The church may have been built on the site of the original Celtic tribal base. The seating plan for the church, drawn up in 1587/88, shows 226 men and women had pews in church, for which they paid varying pew rents.

Interior of Calstock Church. The earliest church at Calstock was built in 1290, but nothing now remains. Part of the present building dates from the fourteenth century, and the whole was extensively restored in 1867 by James St Aubyn when Thomas Hullah was vicar of Calstock. The roof of the aisles and nave is a typical West Country 'wagon' roof.

Gunnislake Church concert, late 1920s. As well as being a social centre, churches gave the opportunity for creative talent. This Church concert demonstrates some wonderful costume making. Ida Collins (later Crossman) is second from the left.

Gunnislake Sunday school concert, late 1920s. Most children went to Sunday school in the pre- and immediate post-war period. In this picture the girl in the centre, marked with a cross, is Velma Collins who was playing the princess. The boy with a cross is Joe Trebilcock.

The superintendent of Mount Zion Sunday school. Mr J.H. Reed was superintendent of the Sunday School for more than sixty years.

Another Sunday school concert, this time at Latchley Chapel in the 1950s. Among those taking part are, middle row, left, Thelma Pridham, right, Jean Pridham and, front right, Wendy McNamara.

Sunday school, Harrowbarrow, *c.* 1890. This appears to be a fiftieth anniversary celebration of the Sunday school at Harrowbarrow Chapel.

Harvest Festival at Tavistock Hotel, Gunnislake, 1950s. Stanley Stephens, owner of Stephens Garage, is checking that everything is ready for the Harvest Festival held in an upstairs room of the Tavistock Hotel. The harvest vegetables and goods were auctioned for charity.

Eight

Music and Festivals

Gunnislake Temperance Band, 1907/08. Singing and music-making started in the chapels, but became a social activity in its own right. Many of the villages had their own bands, a tradition started with brass bands set up by the mines. The Temperance Band was a typical mixture of a social group set up to promote a religious ideal.

Marching band, Chapel Street, Gunnislake, 1900. A crowd has gathered to watch this band playing as they march down Chapel Street in Gunnislake. They are standing in front of Mr Pendry's hardware store, now the site of Gunnislake car park.

Cantata at Gunnislake, 1909. This delightful picture taken beside the Newbridge Chapel at Gunnislake includes a little boy who is rather incongruously carrying a rifle. The floral head-dresses of the girls and women, and the buttonholes of the men makes it look like a wedding, but the hand-written title, 'Cantata at Gunnislake' shows that the occasion was some sort of singing event. The reason for the event is now forgotten, as is the reason why the little boy in the front row is holding a rifle. As so often in such pictures, the outfits worn give no hint of the poverty of the families in Gunnislake at this time, with mining pretty well at an end. Money was regularly put aside to pay for smart clothes such as these for special occasions.

Opposite below: Gunnislake Brass Band. Gunnislake's band met in a room at the Orchard in Gunnislake, near the modern doctor's surgery. From left to right, back row: B. Haddy, -?-, F. Leseelleur, -?-, P. Short, Mr Haddy, Mr Cann. Middle row: -?-, C. Hill, C. Rodda, -?-, -?-, A. Woolcock, L. Rodda, P. Moyle. Front row: C. Crocker, E. Trewin, -?-, H. Trewin, B. Westlake, -?-.

Calstock Quintet. Like so many industrial areas, singing, in choirs or small groups, became an extremely popular pastime. Women got used to hearing their men singing in beautiful harmonies as they walked home from the pub at the weekend. Groups used to gather at 'Turnpike' (St Ann's Chapel) to sing together, and then leave for their homes, singing as they went. The Calstock Quintet is a more formal singing group, consisting of Bill Murton, Bill Reynolds, Hartley Preston, Hubert Foster and George Craddick.

Gunnislake Male Voice Choir, 1937. Men would meet in rooms above the Tavistock Hotel to sing together. This choir has won the Lady Astor Cup. From left to right, back row: H. Jane, Stan Williams, Les Sims, Jim Haddy, Fred Higman, Alf Woolcock, Jack Pine, Charlie Tucker, Albert Rowse, Frank Quick. Middle row: Noel Hunn, Les Dingle, Tom Snell, Jim Higman, Frank Haddy, Lou Bond, Bob Smith, Jack Sleep, Gerald Hunn, Alf Morcom. Front: Garfield Hunn, Tommy Voswill, Peter Jones, Ken Tremain, Charles Millman (conductor), Claude Tremain, Dick Haddy, Russell Westlake, Charles Harris, Harry Cowl.

A horse-drawn carnival float, early twentieth century. The annual carnival gave villagers another opportunity to dress up. Each village had its own carnival; nowadays Calstock is the only place to have something similar at its annual May revels. This horse-drawn wagon shows how the idea of a carnival float developed.

Harrowbarrow Carnival, early twentieth century. The horse has been decorated to pull this carnival float, which seems rather like a series of advertisements, through Harrowbarrow. In the driver's seat is Bill Launder, with Olive Bray and Kath Lampen behind.

Carnival crowd at Harrowbarrow Square, late 1940s. This crowd has gathered outside the post office to watch the carnival procession. From right to left are Dick Congdon, Bert Gileron, -?-, Joyce Jarvis (née Collins), Nancy Symons, -?-, Eileen Vanstone, June Congdon, Bill Symons, Gladys Pooley (née Launder), Elsie Hunn, 'Gran' Geneva Rich, Mrs Hunn, Pearl Launder, Ann Elias (née Lane), Caroline Coles.

Women's Institute float at Gunnislake Carnival, 1930s. Of all the carnivals, the one at Gunnislake was probably the biggest event, although the busy modern road that runs through the village prevents a modern carnival. This picture includes Louie Trebilcock, Olive Lake, Mabel Watkins (above the sign), Clara Oliver (centre), Mrs Conium (under parasol on far right), Mrs Veal, Mrs Rooke and Mrs Williams (front row).

The start of the procession, 1950s. Before today's traffic made it impossible, Gunnislake Carnival procession used to gather on the Devon side of Newbridge before parading across the bridge, up Newbridge Hill and through Gunnislake and other villages. Here Bill Trebilcock and Joe Francis wait for the off.

Gunnislake Carnival Queen, 1939. Velma Collins was the last Carnival Queen before the war. She is about to be crowned by the WI president, Miss Stumbles. From left to right: Jean Chapman, Olive Weeks, Miss Stumbles, Velma Collins, Mr Horiban (Liberal MP), Olive Lake, and shopkeeper George Bolt.

Crowd watching Gunnislake Carnival, 1950s. A huge crowd gathered each year to watch the carnival. Among the faces are Hazel Southcott, Sybil Gibson, Terrell Sutton, Joyce Barnett, Stella Barnett, Olive Sutton, Mr and Mrs Tremaine, Hilda Collins, Mrs Moyle, Annie Penny,

Mrs Martin, Mrs Sanders, Phyllis and Ian Lavers, Mrs Doidge, Janie Viant, Dots Hayward, Mrs Crowell, Cyril Chamings, Mrs Jury, Jimmy Richards, Jack Dure, Harry Hambly, Gwen Rice and Freda Raxworthy.

Party at Gunnislake Village Hall, 1960s. The Village Hall is still very much a centre of community life, particularly for the older folk, and for children's events. This Christmas party includes, from left to right, front row: one of the Dolly sisters, -?-, -?- , Mrs Strong, -?-, Bessie Sanders, Mrs Trelease, Mrs Gibson, Mrs Hodge, another of the Dolly sisters. Middle row: Mrs Allen, Mrs Howe, Miss Drown, Mrs Rodda, Mrs Soper, Mrs Ivy Higman, -?-, Mrs Short, Mrs Trewin, -?-, -?-, Mrs Standing, -?-, -?-, -?-, Mrs Penny, -?-, Mrs Venning, Mrs Stevens, Mrs Richards, Mr Penny, Mrs Chapman, Mrs Secombe, Mrs Cory and Mrs Rook. Back row: -?-, -?-, -?-, Mr Dyer, ? Alonzo Veal, -?-, -?-, Mrs Took, Mrs Smith.

Harrowbarrow Institute. When the mining boom was at its peak, Harrowbarrow had a miner's club – now Club Cottage. Later the wooden Harrowbarrow Institute was built. From left to right, front row: Stanley Bray, Kathleen Lampen (née Congdon), Olive Bray (née Collings), Lucinda Rich (née Bray), -?-, -?-, -?-, Jim Langsford, Archie Knott, Harriet Smale, Harriet Langsford, Mr Bowden, Olive Hambly (née Spear). Second row: Picky Rich, -?-, Len Spear, -?-, Bessie Langsford, Elsie Langsford, -?-, Susan Eastley, Mrs Parnham, -?-, Alice Gileron, Harriet Smale, Gran Rich, Mrs Matthews, -?-. Third row: -?-, ? Bowden, Jack Lilly, -?-, -?-. Fourth row: Harry Spear, Cyril Wilson, -?-, -?-. Back row: Lewis Eastley, -?-, -?-, Eddie Knott.

Latchley, Chilsworthy and Cox Park Show, 1980s. This small agricultural show was reinstated in 1977 to mark the Silver Jubilee, but villagers remember an annual show taking place in the 1920s and 1930s at the community hall between Latchley and Chilsworthy. Sadly, the sheep show has not been held for the past two years, largely due to restrictions caused by Foot and Mouth disease.

Chilsworthy Minstrels. 'Guising' was an ancient tradition in the Calstock area. 'Here at Calstock the traditional form of popular Christmas expression was known as "darkeying", when groups of all ages would dress up in wierd clothes, blacken their faces with burnt cork and thus greatly contribute to the lively evening, with their music, dancing and carol singing', so wrote Henry James in the Calstock News of 1982. It was part of the Christmas celebrations, when the black-faced singers would knock at doors and entertain – mostly for the price of a mug of ale.

Guisers, Christmas Day, c. 1990. In Calstock the guising tradition has been revived. To be more politically correct the musicians have reverted to the older, original name of 'guisers' (from disguise). At some time in the 1980s they were asked to accompany Father Christmas on his Christmas Day visit to the Village Hall, and another custom was started. From the left: Simon Ball, Malcolm Baldwin, Hilary Coleman, Kes Tagney, Jo Tagney, Neil Gallcher, Patrick Coleman, Will Coleman, David Wyatt.

Calstock Giant, May Revel, 1991. Each year the giant Tavy is accompanied by a motley crew of musicians and dancers on the May Bank Holiday to the 'Calstock May Revel' tune. Once on the Quay, the local schoolchildren re-enact the legend of Tavy and Tamara, and the mummers re-interpret an old Cornish mummer's play to illustrate a more modern theme. At the end of the day Tavy sails away down the river accompanied by a 'Farewell Shanty'.

Nine
Royal Events

Flags fly in Fore Street, Calstock, to mark the Coronation of Edward VII, 1902.

The Prince of Wales visits Gunnislake, 1911. This and the following picture were taken on the first visit of Edward, Prince of Wales to his Cornish properties after his father, George V, came to the throne in 1910. The future Edward VIII often passed through Gunnislake on his way to and from the Duchy Farm at Stoke Climsland and other properties belonging to the Duchy of Cornwall.

Here the Royal motorcade seems to have a reason to stop at the derelict Mrs Tooks' lodging house, once a home to tramps and vagrants. In 1918 on his visit to the mines of Kit Hill and Clitters, he walked through the woods back to his car here beside Newbridge. Note the gas light on the right.

Silver Jubilee milk float, Gunnislake, 1977. Jo Hall, with her first electric milk float, which was pulled by hand, and is here decorated to celebrate the Queen's Silver Jubilee. She is the granddaughter of the Hall family of Ferry Farm, opposite Calstock village, who were dairy farmers.

Golden Jubilee milk float, 2002. Twenty-five years later, Jo Hall is still running her milk round in Gunnislake. The modern electric float is decorated again to celebrate Elizabeth II's reign.

Silver Jubilee street party, Gunnislake, 1977. The Silver Jubilee was one of the last occasions to see the large street parties that had been held to celebrate events in the previous fifty years. By the Golden Jubilee, people chose different ways to celebrate the event.

King George VI inspecting Calstock, Gunnislake and Harrowbarrow Home Guard, 1941. The job of the Home Guard in an area twenty miles north of badly blitzed Plymouth was quite important. Platoons from a large area gathered at Stoke Climsland Church for this visit by King George VI.

Ten

The Second World War

VE Day, Albaston, 1945. During the Blitz, people living in the Calstock villages were witnesses to the heavy bombing of Plymouth, twenty miles to the south. Many people moved out of the city, and took shelter where they could – hen houses on Hingston Down and railway huts were preferable to the risk of bombing. So the news of victory was greatly celebrated. This picture of celebrations at Albaston shows how few of the young men were in the village at the time.

VE Day, Delaware, 1945. Villagers from Chilsworthy joined a celebration at Delaware School, where, among other things, a fancy dress football match was held.

VE Day tea party, Gunnislake, 1945. This party was held at the Orchard, now demolished and the location of the Doctors' surgery in the village. From left to right, back row: Mrs Raxworthy, Mrs Pote, Mrs Crowl, Mrs Paddon, -?-, Mrs Southcott, Mrs Brailey, Mrs Williams, Mrs Bratchley, Mrs Lavers, -?-, Mrs Allen, Dorothy Venning, Mr Paddon, Mr. Crowl, -?-. Seated, back row: Gloria Thompson, Maureen Pote, -?-, -?-, Jean Kerslake, Pauline Stone, -?-, Margaret Davy, Pam Southgate, -?-, Edith Paddon. Seated front: John Williams, -?-, John Crowl, Francis Brailey, James Ninnim, Derek Bratchley, -?-, ? Sanders, John Southcott, Derek Smith, ? Kerslake, ? Kerslake, Gerald Brailey.

Concert party at Gunnislake 1940/41. This special concert was held in Gunnislake Public Hall to encourage people to join the National Savings Scheme, and 'Look for the Silver Lining'. From left to right, back row: Len Cory, B. Manning. Middle row: Sam Folly, M. Cook, V. Cook, L. Allen, P. Chapman, J. Chapman, Agnes Haddy, V. Ninnim. Front row: G. Friendship, H. Kemp.

Phil Radford in his demob suit, Calstock, 1945. Everyone stopped to have a chat with Phil Radford when he returned from war, and walked down Fore Street in Calstock wearing his smart demob suit.

Home Guard at Delaware school. The Home Guard met regularly at the new Delaware School building during the Second World War. The headmaster of the secondary school, Mr Johns, fifth from the left on the bottom row, was in charge of the platoon. Many of the young men in the Home Guard were local farmers, exempted from service to keep the country fed. The market gardens of the Calstock area were particularly useful for providing the fruit and vegetables that could no longer be imported, and some local farmers were encouraged to rip up their daffodil fields to plant potatoes. The Home Guard in this picture were trained to defend New Bridge at Gunnislake, and people still remember the anti-tank measures that were set up at the bottom of New Bridge Hill. Front row: Joe Johns (third from left), Sid Johns (fifth from left), Fred Weekes, Albert Rowse, Fred Cook, ? Woolcock, Les Rundle (seventh to eleventh from left). Second Row: Les Woolcock (left), Jack Dodd, Doug Woolcock, ? Wakeham, Jim Lawrence, Alonzo Veale (sixth to tenth from left). Back Row: Frank Rowse, Tom Sobey, Morley Rogers (fifth to seventh from left).

Eleven
Sports and Outings

Latchley school football team, 1920. Most villages of the parish had their own football teams. The players in this school side went on to great success in Chilsworthy Football Club, encouraged initially by their teacher, Beryl Stenlake, who among her other duties, taught them sport. From left to right, back row: George Reynolds, Sean Richards, Lesley Neal. Middle row: Charles Sobey, Albert Allen, Eric Rogers, Tom Sobey. Front row: Fred Dodd, Frank Uglow, Morley 'Star' Rogers, Sidney 'Dinks' Pridham, Gerald Pridham.

Chilsworthy Football Team, 1938. In the thirties, Chilsworthy was one of the most successful teams in the parish, winning many local cups, including, in 1938, the Bedford Cup. Spectators would pay 2d to watch their matches, which took place in a field beside Darkey Lane. From left to right, back row: Reg Woolcock, -?-, Fred Stacey, George Reynolds, Mr Hocking, B. Rogers, Hecky Sullivan, Gordon Haddy, Pastor Frost, Sam James. Middle row: Mr Woodman, Morley Rogers, Heather and Dick Pengelly, Tom Collins. Front row: Norman Honey, George Burleigh, Eric Burley, Eric Pethick, Silvey Forbes.

Calstock School Football Team, 1924. More budding footballers who started their interest while at school. This photograph, taken at the back of the school building, includes, from left to right, front row: ? Mountjoy, Reg Studden, Len Philp (captain), Harold Fletcher, Harold Studden. Middle row: Jim Royston, Harold Coombe, Henry Barrett. Back row: Cecil Start, Stan Pontin, Norman Martin.

Calstock Football Team, 1950s. From left to right, front row: Keith Conium, Doug Reed, Paul Walters, Len Walsh. Back row: Brian Pengelly, Derek Johns, John Moyle, Jeff Wilton, Ted Martin, Arthur Channon, Stan Talbot.

Calstock football team winning the Bedford Cup, 1961. Paul Walters is receiving the Bedford Cup after a successful season from Bill Short, who was goalkeeper for Plymouth Argyle and the Welsh international side. Behind is Harry Rowse.

Football Team, Metherell. Another keen side. Front row: -?-, John Hunn, ? Isobel, Garfield Cundy, -?-. Middle row: Aubrey Cundy, ? Langsford, -?-. Back row: -?-, -?-, Sidney Trewartha, Natus Stephens, Murphy Sleeman.

St Ann's Chapel Football Team.

Gunnislake Cricket Club, 1921. Cricket was also a popular pastime. On the right of the front row is Gwen Rice, and behind her on her right is Jimmy Short. Henry Terrell, the umpire, is at the back on the right.

Calstock Regatta, 1900. Small boats as well as barges were a common sight on the Tamar when it was used as a thoroughfare rather than a barrier, and informal races between the rowers must have led to more formal regattas. The 18ft licensed watermen's boats gradually evolved into the flash boats used for racing at regattas. Although the watermen worked their boats single-handedly with one pair of paddles, the four-oared, coxed men's races have become the high point of every regatta. Roundabouts and a carnival are on the bank for this regatta, which is being viewed by spectators in rowing boats waiting to cheer on the flash boats. Crowds are also thronging the decks of the barges moored along the quays.

Calstock Regatta, 1960s. This photograph was taken from the viaduct and shows the activity on shore as well as on the water. The regattas were revived around this time after a lapse of about two decades following the Second World War. The rowing club still attracts many youngsters from the village into the various crews, and the regatta is still held every year in June or July according to the dictates of the available tides.

Swimmers at Weir Head, Gunnislake, c. 1930. The 'Island' at Gunnislake, by the lock-keeper's cottage, was a popular place for camping and picnicking, and the river at the weir was used for swimming. It is thought these men are workers from Devonport dockyard enjoying themselves at Weir Head.

A day out for the employees of the Western Counties and General Manure Company Ltd in 1915. In Victorian times, when outings were mainly on a horse-drawn cart, people from Calstock had to be content with local trips, but once the motorized charabanc became popular, destinations such as Torbay, Looe and in this case Newquay became popular. The driver sat in the middle seat at the front, often with his 'best girl' on one side and her mother on the other. Among the men standing are Tom Olds (fourth from left) with Fred Williams in front with a coat over his arm.

Outing from Harrowbarrow, 1920s. Often a musician would accompany the charabanc trip; in this case Charlie Sandercock is seated at the back with his accordion. Iris White is seated next to the driver, with Gran Rich behind her sitting next to Mrs Millett. In the fourth row are Mr and Mrs Earl. Bill Matthews and Bill Flats are the two little boys in straw hats in the middle of the charabanc, and Sid, Alf and Jack Cook are standing at the back.

Stephens Gunnislake bus trips, 1950s. By the Second World War, bus trips had replaced the place of the open charabanc trips, and in this case the outing was just for the men, of whom several seem to be enjoying a bottle of beer. The Stephens family ran three buses from their garage in Gunnislake.

Twelve
Schools

The inside of Latchley School in the 1950s. This class, including Thelma Pridham, Wendy Johns, Jean Pridham, Roger Rowse, Ronald Hickman, Peter Coles, Dawn Woolcock and Wendy McNamara, are working studiously under their teacher, Miss Baker. But the school's punishment book reveals what would happen if they were disobedient – strokes with a ruler were not uncommon, and one unlucky boy got six strokes in March 1952 when his misdemeanours were recorded for the third time in as many months. After the Second World War uncertainty hung over Latchley school, and teachers seldom stayed very long. With numbers down to twenty-four, Latchley school closed in 1956, and the children were transferred to Delaware school.

Latchley School, c. 1920. A new building was provided for Latchley school in 1891, after thirty years spent in the former chapel in Latchley village itself. The new building, situated halfway between Latchley and Chilsworthy, cost more than £900 and was built by Isaac Rosekilly of Albaston. It was sorely needed. In 1876, 214 children were on the school's books, crammed into a tiny building.

Latchley schoolchildren 1896. These children were enjoying the new school premises, but even then the need for extra hands at harvest time and inclement weather often prevented children from attending. The school logbook for 13 November 1894 is one example: 'Latchley Bridge was washed away last night, and the children from that side cannot attend.' This photograph is of the twenty-three children in the infant department, with the headmistress Maria George, and their teacher Amy Down. Some names include: Mary Maria Stacey (second row, second from right) with Leonora and Victoria Hearn on her right, a little girl from the Jenkins family on the left of that row and May Sennett second from the right in the front row. The school at the time still had some 111 children on its books.

Churchtown School, Calstock. Calstock had two schools, Churchtown School (near the church) and the National or Board School (in the village). This photograph of Churchtown School was taken in 1935/36, with, from left to right, front row: Ken Pridham, Den Pridham, Ken Vowden, Herbert Vowden, Norman Trewartha. Middle row: Mrs Amery, Jim Pengelly, Eunice Pridham, Thona Pridham, Daisy Ford, Rita Bolt, Sid Vowden, Mrs Foster. Back row: Rosie Hillman, Mavis Bolt, Helen Hillman. The children came from several villages around to attend the school.

Calstock Board School, 1896. The school board which ran the school at the time rented rooms from the old Mount Zion Chapel trustees, and children spent Sundays at Sunday school in the same place. This photograph of 1896 includes Edith Olds (bottom right) and Kate Olds (back, centre), with their teacher Miss Glanville.

Gunnislake School, 1939. Back row: -?-, -?-, C. Bratchley, Betty Woolcock, Doreen Southcott, Betty Smith, Mary Trudgeon, M. Turner, Teacher: Miss Risden. Third row: B. Marsh, -?-, Joyce Marks, Elsie Ferris, Agnes Haddy, Pearl Penrose, Muriel Soper, Pam Southcott, Joan Howe. Second row: Ray Sanders, -?-, D. Hill, Len Cory, B. Ninnim, P. Cross, -?-. Front row: J. Wakeham, S. Williams, P. Walley, G. Chave, -?-, J. Avery.

Thirteen

Shops and Commerce

Southern Railway Carrier, c. 1930. Jack and Wilfred Pine are standing in front of the sort of truck used as a carnival float outside their home on Calstock Road.

Stephen's Garage, Gunnislake, *c.* 1920. Nowadays it would be impossible to stop in the centre of Gunnislake to fill up with petrol – the subsequent traffic jam would lead to badly frayed tempers. When cars were scarce, the Stephens family set up their garage on Newbridge Hill. A car repair garage still occupies the premises.

Garage and Newbridge Hill, 1950s. Car ownership started to grow after the Second World War, but the heavy traffic now common in the centre of Gunnislake could not be imagined at that time.

Kingdon's Groceries, April 1966. Clarence Kingdon shows off the Mini offered as a prize in a competition run by Danish Bacon. The shops in this picture are now private houses.

Stephens' coaches, Gunnislake, 1950s. From left to right: Marcus Woolcock, Jack Pine, Stan Stephens.

Cyril Jeffery and his twenty-eight-year old horse, Madam, in the 1950s. Cyril Jeffery was still using his horse-drawn van to deliver bread into the 1960s. At the same time he was advertising his modern 'Electric Bakery' on the side of the van!

Opposite below: Trefry shop, Gunnislake, early 1900s. This picture gives a feeling of the packaged goods available in a general store in the early twentieth century. Shops flourished as Gunnislake developed during the mining boom of the mid-nineteenth century, but by this time money was scarce. The modern Gunnislake has very few shops, and the shopkeepers watch potential customers driving past on their way to supermarkets in Tavistock and Callington.

Fore Street, Gunnislake, early twentieth century. Gunnislake at the start of the twentieth century was a thriving village, with at least forty-six shops including jewellers, tailors, ironmongers and a shop selling paraffin, logs and coal. There are no pavements, and very little traffic. Compare that with the modern street, which forms a main route between Devon and Cornwall, complete with traffic lights and traffic jams.

Reg Lock's sale day, Gunnislake, 1950s. Queues built up for the start of the sale at Reg Lock's Stores. From the left in the front of the picture: Eileen Trebilcock, Reg Lock, -?-, Mrs Lavers, -?-, -?-, Mrs Walley, Edna Hunn, Mary Worth, Sandra Blatchford, -?-, Victor Dunn. At the back in front of the window are Mrs Wakeham and Mrs Harewood.

Albaston bakery horse and cart, 1920s. Skinnard's bakery in Albaston had another familiar horse and cart delivering goods around the area.

Harrowbarrow village shop, early 1900s. The Wilton family ran this 'general store and newsagent' in Harrowbarrow in the early part of the twentieth century.

Commercial Hotel, Gunnislake, and guests, *c.* 1950. Many of the pubs and inns around the parish started life as hotels – operating as miners' hostels as the mining boom started, offering lodging while builders quickly put up cottages to cope with the rapidly expanding population. Here, the regulars at the Commercial Hotel have ventured away from the bar for this photograph.

Commercial Street, Calstock, *c.* 1910. The now defunct Commercial Hotel is still remembered in the name of Commercial Street. The buildings to the right of the picture housed the local smithy, where the smith could turn his hand to making any tool or object demanded by mining, farming or shipping. Until a few years ago, the old circular block used in putting iron rims on wooden wheels was still visible sunk into the road opposite.

Fore Street, Calstock, c. 1900. Calstock was reckoned to be one of the best shopping centres in the locality and it was said that anything could be purchased there. Bickles eventually became Cass the drapers, whose lovely brass windowsills still grace the current village general stores. The shop at the far end was a grocer, at one time belonging to Worth, but now incorporated into the Boot Inn.

Fore Street, Calstock, 1907. The restaurant on the right was always known as The Galleon and although now a private residence, is still called Galleon House. Until very recently the remains of the raised lettering for Fry's Chocolate could be seen on the window of the door. The sender of this postcard wrote: 'I am getting on grand just about made my fortune working from 6.30 to 7.30 every day. I go [to] the Wesleyan Chapel'.

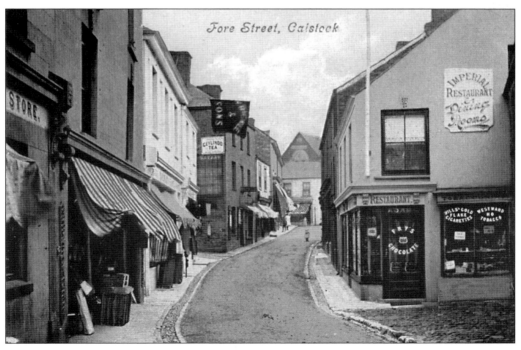

Bickle & Son, Calstock and Gunnislake, *c.* 1900. These two photographs show two shops run by the Bickle family. The one at Calstock (*above*), is now a private house. It could be that the upstairs windows were originally bricked in to avoid window tax – in 1825, houses with fewer than eight windows were exempt from the tax. The refreshments offered were presumably to attract the many day trippers who arrived on the river steamers. The family went on to open an outfitters and milliners in Gunnislake, (*below*).

St Ann's Chapel Post Office, c. 1920. The surface of the road by the time of this photograph has been properly made up. The Post Office and General Stores is on the opposite side of the road to the modern shop.

St Ann's Chapel garage, c. 1920. The garage, unlike the Post Office, has stayed in the same place, although the petrol pumps have changed considerably.

Horse and cart at Little Dale Farm, Latchley. Tractors were still a rarity in Calstock parish until after the Second World War. Carts like this one were used to carry milk churns, and market garden produce to the trains, and the practice continued into the 1950s, even when mechanisation had come to the fields. Valerie Pridham is seated in the cart.

The Queen's Head at Albaston with Skinnard's Bakery in the background, 1930s. The bakery burnt down in 1947, and today the building is used as an old people's home.

Fourteen

Village Scenes, Events and Characters

View across Fore Street, Gunnislake, *c.* 1930. At the height of mining, the hillside opposite Gunnislake was bare, with all available wood being cut down to help fuel the steam pumps, or used for supports for equipment. But it did not take long for the woodland to establish itself once more. The rooftops of Gunnislake are in good condition at this time, and the village shows none of the signs of deterioration that dogged its later history. The circus used to be a regular visitor to the site in the middle foreground, where swings can be seen in this picture.

Gunnislake flooding, 1954. On Friday 26 November 1954, a 'wall of water' crashed down on Gunnislake, according to newspaper headlines the following day. In this newspaper photograph, Horace Southcott is clearing up the mess. Thirty-eight houses were damaged when a leat near a mine at Chilsworthy Beam burst its banks, pouring through Chilsworthy, Dimson and Gunnislake as it fought its way to the Tamar. A wall of Gunnislake school held the water back for a while, but when the wall collapsed, houses in Orchard and Carpenter Streets and Bond's Hotel were flooded. In a matter of minutes, one house was 4ft deep in water. The flooding followed a severe storm that caused damage across the area.

Fallen trees in Greenscombe Woods. The date of the storm that felled these trees in Greenscombe Woods is not known, but the damage could well have been done by the 1954 storm that caused flooding in Gunnislake. Dulcie Pridham stands in the midst of the chaos.

Aerial view of Gunnislake, 1980s. A large number of new houses have been built in Gunnislake in the past fifty years, including these new homes built in the 1980s.

O'Connell's Garage, Newbridge, c. 1940. The garage was built in the 1930s when the original five-storey building was demolished. The building was advertised for sale in 1811 as a newly built granary, but fourteen years later was advertised again as 'The Tamar Brewery and Shrubbery' including a brewery, dwelling house and malt house, with a water wheel. Sometime after 1839 it became a paper mill, using peat to make paper. It caught fire in 1866, when the peat added to the inferno. It was rebuilt with a fifth storey, and provided sixteen lodging tenements for miners and their families, named the Caledonia or Klondike. When the mining boom ended it became Mrs Tooks' lodging house for tramps and vagrants.

Gunnislake Bridge crash, 1937. A lorry load of paving slabs lost control coming down the Devon side and just missed the Tollhouse. The accident has brought onlookers from the village.

Gunnislake from Pearson's Quarry. By the time this picture was taken, the hillside opposite the village had become heavily wooded once more.

Dimson, Gunnislake, *c.* 1920. The distinctive round shape of Plymouth Brickworks can be seen above the neat terraced cottages of Dimson.

View across Gunnislake, *c.* 1920. In the middle distance is a terrace of cottages at Crocker's Row, complete with a standard feature of Victorian and early twentieth century life – outside toilets. At the bottom of the picture, the chimney of the Gasworks can just be seen, with Snowden's Quarry in the middle of the right-hand side.

Gunnislake New Bridge, 1905. This view of Gunnislake, taken from the Devon bank, shows the rows of miners cottages built on the hillside above Newbridge. The river banks that in this picture are completely clear are now shrubby and wooded. Sources of wood were heavily used during the mining era, and the Duke of Bedford who owned the land was keen to keep the banks clear to make fishing easier.

Gunnislake from Weir Head, 1930s. The lock-keepers cottage on the 'Island' can be clearly seen, and behind it the derelict bone mill, once used for making fertilizers.

Calstock plus lime kilns and market gardens. The arches of the lime kilns at Calstock can be clearly seen in this view from the Devon bank. Lime was essential to agriculture and horticulture in the parish from the sixteenth century, as it was used to sweeten the acidic soil. Earlier, sand was brought up by barge from south Cornish beaches to be spread on the land, giving names like Sandhill and Sandquay to places in the area. Market gardens can be seen on the hillside behind the village.

The Tamar frozen over, 1962. These children are enjoying an unexpected game on the Tamar at Calstock during the last 'big freeze' which left much of the area struggling with heavy snow for several weeks.

Calstock foreshore, 1900. The yard in front of the Tamar Inn was often filled with piles of wood brought in from the Baltic. The ground at this time was less muddy than it is now and a swimming club was formed. (Each year the Tamar claimed the bodies of several non-swimmers.) Swimming from this point continued until the 1980s. Bickle's shop is behind the Tamar Inn, and there is no sign of the viaduct or Mount Zion Church. This photograph provides a wonderful glimpse of the quay, with horse-drawn vehicles and children in their everyday clothes.

Lower Kelly Cottages, c. 1950. Calstock viaduct towers over the cottages that lead to the old quays along the waterfront.

Church Street, Calstock, early 1900s. It is amazing to think that the eleven buildings shown here housed seventeen families in the mid-1800s. It is even more amazing that the District Council wanted to pull them down in the 1960s and '70s and were only prevented by strong local action.

CHURCH STREET, CALSTOCK.   7679

Harewood House ruins, *c*. 1920. The Harewood estate was bought by the Trelawny family from the Footes in 1815, but sold when the fumes from nearby Okel Tor Arsenic Works became unbearable. After the departure of the Trelawnys, Harewood House became a boys' private school, which subsequently burnt down. Many of the local hedges have old bedsteads from the dormitory plugging their gaps. The top storey was then removed, the ground floor refurbished and it became a farmhouse. Eventually it was divided into two, and bears little evidence of its former glory.

An Edwardian outing to Cotehele House, *c*. 1910. These Edwardian visitors to Cotehele House were early sightseers to what is now one of Calstock's most popular attractions. The postcard was sent in 1910 by Rhoda Collings to her mother at Menheniot, reminding her that she would be returning to Menheniot station on the four o'clock motor the following Saturday.

Oast House, Albaston, c. 1970. This was part of Albaston Brewery, run by the wealthy and influential Bowhay family throughout the nineteenth century and into the twentieth. This photograph of the ruined building was taken shortly before it was pulled down.

Picnic at Cotehele, 1950s. Holidays away from home were rare, but large family picnics were greatly enjoyed, and the banks of the Tamar provided many attractive spots for a day out, which nearly always included a dip in its very cold water.

Cottages at Callington Road, Harrowbarrow, early twentieth century. This row of miner's cottages is typical of so many built in the middle of the nineteenth century in every village of the parish.

Harrowbarrow Post Office, 1960s. Harrowbarrow is one of the few villages that has managed to retain its post office and shop until the present day.

Collecting water from Harrowbarrow village pump, early 1900s. This elderly gentleman is collecting his water from the village pump, which was the main source of water until the late 1920s. He is wearing hessian sacks over his shoulders and round his waist – the most common working uniform for market gardeners and farmers of the time.

Horse and cart on the Turnpike at Drakewalls, early twentieth century. The Turnpike road running from Gunnislake to Callington through St Ann's Chapel was built at the end of the eighteenth century; before that the old ridgeway across Hingston Down was the main route. People from villages all around would gather at 'Turnpike' on Sunday evenings for a chance to get together and chat, and perhaps enjoy a little romance.

View across Chilsworthy, 1950s. Chilsworthy was a 'worthig' – land enclosed from Hingston Down for agriculture in the eleventh or twelfth century. Its position close to several mines, quarries and brickworks turned it from a loose hamlet of a few farms into a mining village in the 1850s.

WRVS, or Red Cross, outside Bolts Drapery, Gunnislake. Charity fundraising was carried out enthusiastically in the strongly Methodist villages of Calstock parish. Here, from left to right, are: Mrs W.P. Leverton, Mrs Balkwill, E. Sanders, Mrs Trudgeon, Mrs Haydon, Mrs Balkwill, Lilian Woolcock, Miss Sims.

Albaston, early 1900s. An open leat, or drain, runs beside the road in Albaston. In the distance is the village shop and post office.

The first old age pensioners at Albaston, 1909. There must have been quite a sense of occasion when these elderly residents posed for this photograph. Chairs had been placed across the road at Albaston in front of the post office, and on the edges of the picture the village children are keen to get in on the excitement. On the left-hand side is John Snell Snr, with Granfer and Grandma Snell. The thirty-two solemn faces give away little of what must have been a very happy day. It was 1 January 1909 and they were about to receive their very first pensions from the Post Office. The new 'pensioners' must have come from quite a wide area to collect their money. The 5s a week they received saved many from the indignity of seeking help from the Tavistock Union Poorhouse, or from taking to the roads to wander from village to village looking for a bite to eat. In these early days of the century, tramps were still a common sight in the villages of Calstock, sleeping rough and selling odds and ends to make a penny or two.